THE GREAT OUTDOORS

FLY FISHING

Revised and Updated

by **Ellen Hopkins**

Consultant:
Matt Wilhelm
Education Coordinator
Federation of Fly Fishers

Capstone
press®
Mankato, Minnesota

Edge Books are published by Capstone Press,
151 Good Counsel Drive, P.O. Box 669, Mankato, Minnesota 56002.
www.capstonepress.com

Library of Congress Cataloging-in-Publication Data
Hopkins, Ellen.
Fly fishing / by Ellen Hopkins.—Rev. and updated.
p. cm.—(Edge Books. The great outdoors)
Includes bibliographical references and index.
ISBN-13: 978-1-4296-0819-0 (hardcover)
ISBN-10: 1-4296-0819-6 (hardcover)
1. Fly fishing—Juvenile literature. I. Title. II. Series.
SH456.H67 2008
799.12'4—dc22   2007010771

Editorial Credits
Carrie Braulick, editor; Katy Kudela, photo researcher; Jenny Krueger, revised edition
editor; Thomas Emery, revised edition designer; Kyle Grenz, revised edition
production artist

Photo Credits
Bob Pool/TOM STACK & ASSOCIATES, 6, 23
Capstone Press/Gary Sundermeyer, 5, 9, 15, 16, 19, 20, 30, 40
Digital Stock/Marty Snyderman, 10
Jeff Foott/TOM STACK & ASSOCIATES, 13
Loren Irving/Gnass Photo Images, 37
Photo Network, B. Dodge, 25, 26; Stephen Saks, 33
Photri-Microstock, 39
Shutterstock/Geir Olav Lyngfjell, cover
Timothy Halldin, 29
Unicorn Stock Photos/Joe Sohm, 35
Visuals Unlimited, 42; Bernd Wittich, 45
William H. Mullins, 43, 44

1 2 3 4 5 6 12 11 10 09 08 07

TABLE OF CONTENTS

Essential content terms are highlighted and are defined at the bottom of the page where they first appear.

Chapter 1

FLY FISHING

Learn about the history of fly fishing and common freshwater and saltwater fish.

Fly fishing can be a relaxing day at the river or an exciting day at the ocean. Like other kinds of fishing, it requires a reel and a line. But a fly fisher's rod is specially made for fly fishing, and the line has a fly attached to the end of it. A fly is a kind of artificial lure. Fly fishing involves techniques that have worked since ancient times and are popular even today.

History of Fly Fishing

In prehistoric times, people fished to survive. They used darts, spears, or nets. They also used small pointed pieces of wood, bone, or stone called gorges. They covered the gorges with bait and attached them to a line. They may have attached the line to a rod made of wood. A gorge stuck in a fish's throat after the fish swallowed it. People then used the line or rod to bring the fish out of the water.

Not only is fly fishing fun to do with other people, it's also safer that way.

Some historians believe fly fishing began in the area that is now Macedonia. This country is located in southeastern Europe. A book from about AD 200 explains how Macedonians made flies out of wool and feathers. They cast the flies into the water to catch fish.

In later years, fishing was no longer necessary for people's survival. But people still fished to add variety to their diets and for recreation. Today, fly fishing is a popular North American sport. People fly fish with a large variety of flies made of materials such as animal hair, feathers, and cork.

Common Fish

Fly fishers in North America fish for a variety of fish species. Freshwater fish live in streams, rivers, ponds, and lakes. Saltwater fish live in the seas and ocean.

Freshwater
- bass
- crappies
- perch
- pike
- sunfish
- trout
- landlocked salmon
- Atlantic salmon*
- Pacific salmon*

Saltwater
- barracuda
- blue fish
- bonefish
- mackerel
- permit
- shad
- tarpon
- tuna

*Atlantic and Pacific salmon that live in salt water travel to freshwater rivers and large streams to spawn.

species—a group of animals with similar features

spawn—to lay eggs

Foil-Wrapped Trout

Serves: 1   Children should have adult supervision.

Ingredients:
1 tomato
1 medium onion
1 lemon
1 trout fillet (boneless)
1 teaspoon (5 mL) lemon juice
Salt and pepper, as desired
2 1/2 teaspoons (12.5 mL) chopped
   garlic, or as desired

Equipment:
Sharp knife
Aluminum foil
Metal spatula

1. Cut tomato and onion into thin slices.

2. Cut lemon into wedges.

3. Place fish fillet on a large piece of aluminum foil.

4. Sprinkle fish with lemon juice and salt and pepper.

5. Add slices of tomato, onion, and chopped garlic.

6. Fold the foil tightly around the fish and cook on a grill, over a campfire, or in an oven preheated to 325 degrees Fahrenheit (160 degrees Celsius). Turn the fish over with a metal spatula after about 10 minutes. A fish fillet that is about 12 inches (30 centimeters) long usually is fully cooked after about 20 minutes. Fish is fully cooked when it is hot in the center. Serve with lemon wedges.

EDGE FACT —◦–◎

Mako sharks swim faster than any other, and they can even leap out of the water.

Most people think of fly fishing as a relaxing day at a scenic river or lake. But that depends on what you're fishing for. For some brave fly fishers, the ultimate catch is a shark!

Sharks live in saltwater and are fished off coasts around the world. The main attraction for anglers is their size. Off the northeastern coast of the United States, for example, fly fishers face sharks weighing from 100 to 700 pounds (45 to 317 kilograms)!

But sharks are also great fighters and a challenge to reel in. In general, sharks have poor eyesight. So it's hard to attract these monster fish with a fly. But it can be done.

One of the biggest sharks ever caught on a fly was a 600-pound (272 kilogram) mako shark that was 11 feet (3.4 meters) long! According to the angler, the shark was released after a fierce 40-minute fight.

Chapter 2

EQUIPMENT

Learn about types of line, types of flies, and other equipment.

In North America, most freshwater fishers attach live bait or lures to their fishing line. Lures are wood, metal, or plastic objects people use to attract fish. For fly fishers, the lure is the fly. Many fly fishers purchase flies. Some fly fishers make their own flies. This is called fly tying. Fly fishers also use specially made rods, reels, and line for their sport.

Fly Rods

Most fly rods are made of graphite. Fly fishers usually use rods that are about 8.5 to 9 feet (2.6 to 2.7 meters) long. Each fly rod bends in a certain way. This movement is called action. A fly rod's action can be slow, medium, or fast. Slow-action rods are easier for some to cast. Fast-action rods allow fly fishers to cast longer distances than slow- or medium-action rods.

graphite—a strong, lightweight material made from a grey or black mineral

The tackle you use depends on the type of fish you are fishing for.

Fly Reels

Fly rods have reels to hold line. Most reels are made of a lightweight metal called aluminum. Some reels are made of graphite.

People use reels to help them bring in hooked fish. Hooked fish usually run with the line. Fly fishers sandwich the line between their middle finger and the rod to stop the run. Fly fishers then reel in any slack as the fish moves. The fish gradually comes closer as the reel's spool collects line.

Most fly fishers use single-action reels. These reels turn once with each crank of the handle. Other fly fishers use multiplier reels. One crank of the handle turns these reels one and one-half to two times. Multiplier reels are helpful when hooked fish swim long distances with the line.

Most fly reels have a drag system. This system includes a small knob located on the reel's spool or cover. Drag systems slow down the reel's spool or cover to adjust the amount of drag. They help fly fishers control the line.

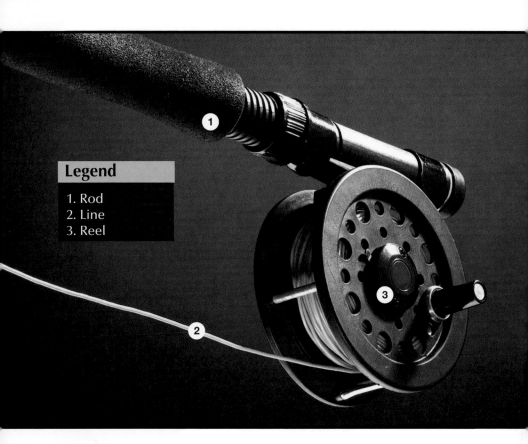

Fly Line

Fly fishing line is called fly line. It is made of a combination of materials such as Dacron and vinyl. Dacron is a manufactured fiber. Most fly lines are 90 feet (27 meters) long. Fly line is thicker and heavier than other fishing line. In bait and lure fishing, the weight of the bait or lure helps pull line off the reel during a cast. But lightweight flies cannot pull line off the reel. Heavy line helps during casting.

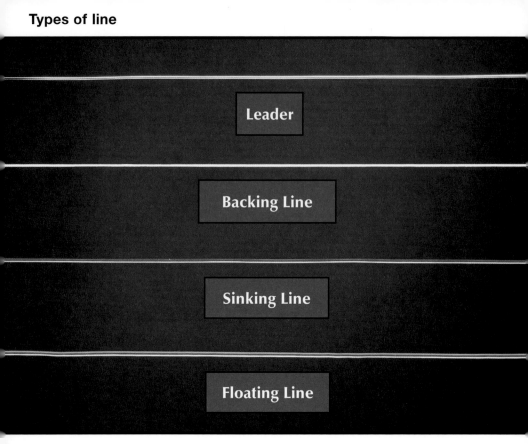

Leader

Backing Line

Sinking Line

Floating Line

Fly line comes in different weights. No. 1 fly line is the lightest. The heaviest fly line is No. 12. Most fly fishers use line weights between No. 4 and No. 8 for average freshwater conditions.

Fly line either floats or sinks. Sinking line usually sinks more than 2 feet (.6 meters) below the surface. Some fly line is intermediate. This fly line sinks to about 1 foot (.3 meters) below the surface.

Backing Line and Leaders

Fly fishers put backing line on their reel before the fly line. They attach one end of this braided Dacron line to the reel. They attach the other end to the fly line. Fly fishers may put 25 to 500 feet (7.6 to 152 meters) of backing line on the reel. Backing line allows fly fishers to give a running fish more line. Large fish often run long distances. These fish can break the line if there is not enough of it.

Fly fishers tie a 1- to 30-foot (.3- to 9.1-meter) nylon leader to the other end of the fly line. Leaders are usually made of thin monofilament line.

Most leaders are tapered. The thick end attaches to the fly line. This part is called the butt. The middle part is called the taper. The tip is called the tippet. Tippets usually are 1 to 3 feet (.3 to .9 meter) long. Fly fishers make a knot to tie the fly to the tippet.

Flies

Fly fishers use different fly patterns. Some flies look like insects. Some look like animals fish eat such as small fish, frogs, or salamanders.

taper—to become narrow on one end

Dry flies are one type of fly pattern. These flies look like insects floating on the water's surface. Fly fishers use floating line with dry flies. They cast dry flies onto the water and let them float for a few seconds to attract fish. They recast if a fish does not take the fly. Fly fishers often cast dry flies upstream.

Fly fishers often use dry flies called bass bugs to fish for bass. These flies can be made of a variety of materials such as wood, cork, foam, plastic, or animal hair.

Wet flies are another type of fly pattern. These flies sink. Fly fishers use sinking line with wet flies. Wet flies look like drowned insects or like small fish or other animals living in the water. Fly fishers sometimes slowly drag wet flies upstream to make them appear more life-like.

Some wet flies look like nymphs. Fly fishers may move the line back and forth to imitate the way nymphs move.

Other wet flies are bucktails or streamers. These flies look like minnows or other small fish. Bucktails and streamers have material

nymphs—insects in a stage of development just before they become adults; nymphs live in water.

Fly fishers can twitch the tip of their rod to imitate swimming nymphs, or allow the nymph to drift without movement.

attached to them called wings. Streamers have wings made of feathers. Bucktails have wings made of animal hair.

Fly fishers sometimes use attractor flies. These flies do not look like any specific insect or animal. Fly fishers use attractor flies both on and under the water's surface.

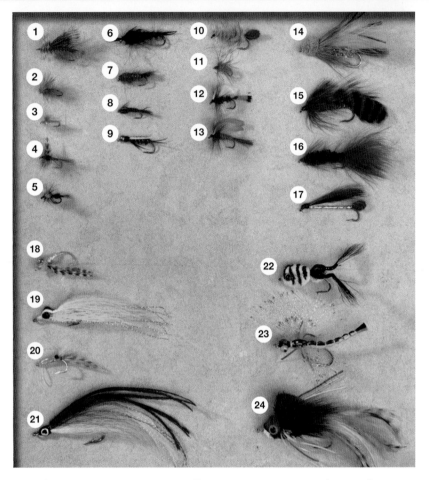

Dry Flies
1. Stimulator
2. Elk Hair Caddis
3. Pale Morning Dun
4. Adams
5. Royal Wulff

Nymphs
6. Black Stonefly
7. Gold-ribbed Hare's Ear
8. Pheasant Tail
9. Bead Head Prince Nymph

Wet Flies
10. Woolly Worm
11. Hare's Ear Soft Hackle
12. Royal Coachman
13. Gold-ribbed Hare's Ear
   with wing

Streamers & Bucktails
14. Marabou Muddler
15. Matuka
16. Wooly Bugger
17. Blacknosed Dace

Saltwater Flies
18. Mini Puff
19. Clouser Minnow
20. Imitator Shrimp
21. Lefty's Deceiver

Bass Bugs
22. Messinger Frog
23. Dragonfly
24. Diving Frog

Some flies are designed to be used in salt water. Many of these flies are streamers. Saltwater flies sometimes look like shrimp, crabs, or minnows.

Hooks

Flies are made by attaching natural and synthetic materials to a hook using a thread. The hooks become caught in a fish's mouth and prevent the fish from escaping. Fly fishers should make sure their hooks are sharp. A sharp hook is more likely to stay in a fish's mouth than a dull hook.

Many fly fishers use hooks without barbs. These sharp points extend from behind a fishhook's point. Barbless hooks cause less damage to the fish.

EDGE FACT

Fly fishers who tie their own flies use detailed patterns and instructions from web sites, magazines, books, and workshops.

synthetic—something made by people rather than found in nature

Other Equipment

Below is some other equipment that fly fishers use for a successful fishing trip.

- **Boxes**—to store flies
- **Chest Waders**—to cover the legs and upper body. Most chest waders have waterproof boots attached to them.
- **Clippers**—to cut line
- **Flashlight**
- **Forceps**—to remove a hook
- **Hat**—with a wide brim to shade the face
- **Hip Boots**—These waders cover fly fishers' legs and have boots attached to them. Hip boots have suspenders that attach to a fisher's belt.
- **Insect Repellent**
- **Net**—to handle a hooked fish
- **Polarized Sunglasses**—to reduce glare and protect the eyes from stray hooks
- **Vests**—with pockets, pouches, and clips to carry fly boxes, line, leaders, and extra flies

Fly fishers should cast toward places that offer food and cover for fish.

A thermometer may also be useful to fly fishers. Some fish are more likely to bite when the water is at a certain temperature. For example, brown trout prefer temperatures that are between 55 and 65 degrees Fahrenheit (13 to 18 degrees Celsius).

Fly fishers should also bring a first aid kit. Fishers can use items in this kit, such as gauze and bandages, to treat injuries.

Chapter 3

SKILLS AND TECHNIQUES

Learn about finding fish, approaching the water, and casting.

Fly fishers use various methods to catch fish. Most fly fishers wade into the water to fish or fish from shore. Some fly fishers fish from boats. Fly fishers should learn about the features and habits of the fish that they are trying to catch.

Reading the Water

Skilled fly fishers know where to find fish. This skill is called "reading the water." Lake fish often move to different areas to search for food. River and stream fish often stay in one place and let the current bring food to them. Fly fishers try to find out which way fish are moving. They watch for fish to rise to the water's surface to eat insects.

EDGE FACT

It is easier to "read" the currents of a river or stream than it is to read a still pool of water. Currents can tell fly fishers where the fish are.

24

If fish stop feeding, take a break for 5 to 10 minutes. This is called "resting" the fish.

Fly fishers look for places where fish are likely to feed. They may fish in a lake's inlet or outlet to a river. Fish often gather in these areas. The water that enters and exits lakes often carries more oxygen and food than other lake areas.

Stream fish often gather in small pools of slow-moving water called pocket water

Fly Fishing—Skills and Techniques

to rest. Rocks, logs, or other structures in the water create pocket water. These objects slow the current's speed by changing its direction.

Fly fishers look for fish in other places. Fish often spend time near visible lines in the water called edges. A row of plants or an area where calm water meets fast water may form edges. Fish often live near fallen logs, large rocks, or sandbars.

The Approach

Fly fishers carefully approach and wade into the water. Fish have good eyesight. They can be startled by objects moving above them. Fly fishers try not to form large or moving shadows over the water. Fly fishers may wear clothing that blends with the surroundings. Some fishing experts believe that bright colors can scare fish away.

Fish can sense vibrations. Fish often sense the vibration of people walking on shore. Fly fishers stay calm and walk into the water slowly. They try not to kick rocks or walk on loose rocks. Large splashes could frighten fish.

edge—a visible line where water changes or plants grow

Fly fishers should stay still for a few moments after they wade into the water. This pause in movement is to help calm any frightened fish.

The Cast

The fly cast has two parts. These parts are the backcast and the forward cast. Fly fishers make the backcast first. They begin with 25 to 30 feet (7.6 to 9.1 meters) of line spread straight out in front of them. Fly fishers grip the rod with their palm facing down. The thumb should lie along the rod's top. Fly fishers keep their wrist tight. They can then pull off some of the line from the reel with their free hand. The amount of line they pull off depends on how far they want to cast.

Fly fishers lift the rod's tip to begin the backcast. They quickly move the rod's tip just past their shoulder. They then stop the movement without bending the wrist. The line should unfold behind them.

Stop backcast at 10 o' clock.

Stop forward cast at 2 o' clock.

Line unfolds.

Bring rod down between shoulder and waist as line unfolds and the fly lands on the water.

Fly fishers begin the forward cast when the line is almost straight behind them. They quickly move the rod forward. They stop the movement just after the rod passes the shoulder. They then let out some line from their free hand. They move the rod down between their shoulder and waist as the line straightens out in front of them.

30 **Fly fishers false cast before they begin fishing.**

Fly fishers sometimes false cast. Fly fishers move quickly from the backcast to the forward cast when they false cast. They keep the line above the water's surface.

People false cast for various reasons. It helps the line slip easily from the reel to the distance needed for the cast. It also can dry out a fly or help fly fishers learn the casting movement.

Chapter 4

CONSERVATION

Learn about protecting habitats, fisheries, and licenses and regulations.

Fish populations are not as large as they once were. Many of the water sources where trout once lived have been polluted or destroyed. Trout can only live in about 15 percent of the waters they once lived in. More than 80 fish species are in danger of dying out.

Fly fishers can protect fish populations and their habitats. Fly fishers should follow the state or province fishing rules. They should also take any trash home with them or place it in trash cans.

EDGE FACT

Some areas have laws against fishing with flies that contain lead. Lead can poison waterfowl and other birds who accidentally ingest it.

habitat—the natural conditions and places where fish live

Fly fishers can help preserve the areas in which they fish.

Conservation Efforts

In 1940, the U.S. government established the U.S. Fish and Wildlife Service. This department restores fish populations and damaged habitats. It also establishes wildlife refuges. Fish, birds, and other animals live in these protected areas.

The U.S. Fish and Wildlife Service oversees the National Fish Hatchery System (NFHS). The NFHS raises fish in hatcheries. These fish are released into water sources to help increase the populations of certain fish.

Fisheries and Oceans Canada (DFO) helps protect and maintain fish habitats in Canada. DFO also maintains fish populations and conducts studies on how climate and other factors affect fish habitats.

Other groups work to restore water sources and fish populations. These groups include the Federation of Fly Fishers, Trout Unlimited, and the Native Fish Conservancy. Members of these groups rebuild gravel beds where fish spawn. Some groups build buffer strips.

buffer strips—strips of land that prevent pollutants from entering water sources

Fish raised in hatcheries can help increase populations of certain fish species.

Fly fishers should release fish that they do not plan to eat. They should release the fish as soon as they remove the hook. They try to keep the fish in the water. Fish quickly run out of oxygen when they are removed from the water.

Fly fishers follow certain steps to release fish. They hold fish underwater for a few seconds to allow them to receive oxygen through their gills. Fish breathe through these openings on their sides. Fly fishers should make sure fish are facing upstream. Fish that are not facing upstream may be carried upside down by the current. They may die because they are unable to flip over.

Licenses and Regulations

Fly fishers need to follow government rules. These rules help protect fish populations. States and provinces require fishers to have a fishing license after they turn a certain age. This age ranges from 12 to 16.

Most people buy full-season licenses. These licenses allow fly fishers to fish in their home state or province throughout the year or fishing season. States and provinces allow fishing during fishing seasons. The length of seasons varies according to the location and fish species. Fly fishers usually need to buy separate licenses or permits when they fish outside of their home state or province.

Be sure to handle fish gently and don't squeeze them. Often if you hold fish belly-up they will relax.

Fly fishers also must follow limit regulations. These rules allow one person to catch a certain number of fish in one day. Limit rules vary by area and fish species. Some states and provinces close rivers to fishing during spawning season.

Chapter 5

SAFETY

Learn about fly fishing safely in different waters and weather conditions.

All water areas can be dangerous. Fly fishers must follow safety guidelines. Safe fishers reduce their chances of injury and are prepared if accidents do occur.

Water Safety

Fly fishers should be careful when they wade into the water. Rocks might be slippery. Currents can be strong. Fly fishers should walk sideways into the current. They should try to avoid deep water and fast-moving shallow water.

Fly fishers in boats should wear life jackets. Life jackets can help fishers survive if their boat tips or if they fall out of the boat.

Weather Safety

Fly fishers should learn the day's weather forecast before they go out to fish. They should watch for approaching thunderstorms as they fish.

Fly fishers in boats must wear life jackets.

Do not wade out past your knees in fast water.

Fly fishers who are caught in storms should quickly get out of the water. They should also stay away from tall trees and ridges. Lightning is more likely to strike these places. Fly fishers should lay down their rods during storms. Graphite fly rods can attract lightning.

Fly Fishing—Safety

Fly fishers should try to stay warm in cold weather. They should add layers of clothing if they become cold. Fly fishers may get hypothermia if they get too cold. This condition occurs when a person's body temperature drops below 95 degrees Fahrenheit (35 degrees Celsius). Hypothermia can cause confusion, fatigue, and even death.

Other Safety Guidelines

Safe fly fishers are careful around others. They look around to make sure no one is nearby when they cast. Beginning fly fishers should fish with another person. Other people can help if an accident occurs.

Fly fishers should know how to use the items in their first aid kits. They then can treat small injuries.

Safe fly fishers take their sport seriously. They are aware of their surroundings and are prepared for accidents. Safe fly fishers set a good example for other participants in the sport.

EDGE FACT

A wading belt helps keep water out of your waders if you fall in.

Tarpon

Description: Tarpon have dark blue to green backs that fade into silver along the fish's sides. They have large scales. Tarpon usually weigh about 45 pounds (20 kilograms). But they can weigh more than 100 pounds (45 kilograms).

Habitat: near river mouths and inlets, bays, offshore waters; young tarpon may live in freshwater

Food: young fish, crabs, shrimp

Flies: Cockroach, Seducer, Purple People Eater, Boca Grande, Homosassa Special, Golden Claw

Smallmouth Bass

Description: Smallmouth bass are green-brown to brown. They have a mouth that extends to the front of the eye. They have dark, broken vertical bands along their sides. Smallmouth bass usually weigh about .5 to 4 pounds (.2 to 1.8 kilograms).

Habitat: deep, cool lakes; rocky, quickly flowing streams

Food: minnows, insects, crawfish, frogs

Flies: nymphs; streamers such as the Woolly Bugger, Marabou Leech, Black Marabou Muddler, and Muddler Minnow

Rainbow Trout

Description: Rainbow trout have silver skin covered with small black spots. A pink-orange band usually runs lengthwise along their sides. Rainbow trout usually weigh about 2 pounds (.9 kilogram).

Habitat: cold, quickly flowing rivers and streams; cold lakes

Food: insects, small fish, fish eggs

Flies: nymphs; dry flies such as the Blue-winged Olive, Royal Wulff, Gray Hackle, and Adams

Atlantic Salmon

Description: Atlantic salmon have silver sides with black spots. They have four or fewer spots on their gill cover. Atlantic salmon usually weigh about 8 to 12 pounds (3.6 to 5.4 kilograms).

Habitat: deep pools of water near rocks and other structures; freshwater streams and rivers during spawning season

Food: small fish

Flies: wet flies such as Thunder and Lightning and Jock Scott; dry flies such as the Royal Wulff

GLOSSARY

buffer strips (BUF-er STRIPS)—strips of land that prevent pollutants from entering water sources

edge (EJ)—a visible line where water changes or plants grow

graphite (GRA-fite)—a strong, lightweight material made from a grey or black mineral

habitat (HAB-uh-tat)—the natural place and conditions in which animals live

hatchery (HACH-er-ee)—a place where people allow fish eggs to hatch

nymphs (NIMFS)—insects in a stage of development just before they become adults; nymphs live in water.

spawn (SPON)—to lay eggs

species (SPEE-shees)—a group of animals with similar features

synthetic (sin-THET-ik)—something that is made by people rather than found in nature

taper (TAY-per)—to come to a point. The middle part of a leader is also called a taper.

READ MORE

Klobuchar, Lisa. *Fishing.* Get Going! Hobbies. Chicago: Heinemann, 2006.

Oglesby, Arthur. *Fly-fishing.* Complete Guide to Fishing. Broomall, PA: Mason Crest, 2003.

Seeberg, Tim. *Flyfishing.* Kids' Guides to the Outdoors. Chanhassen, Minn: Child's World, 2004.

INTERNET SITES

FactHound offers a safe, fun way to find Internet sites related to this book. All of the sites on FactHound have been researched by our staff.

Here's how:

1. Visit *www.facthound.com*

2. Choose your grade level.

3. Type in this book ID **1429608196** for age-appropriate sites. You may also browse subjects by clicking on letters, or by clicking pictures and words.

4. Click on the **Fetch It** button.

FactHound will fetch the best sites for you!

INDEX